Dude, Where's My Childhood?

A Survival Guide for Boys Turning 13 and Beyond

Tammy Friedman

Seaside Serenity Scripts Publishing

Dude, Where's My Childhood

A Survival Guide for Boys Turning 13 and Beyond

Contact: www.seasideserenityscripts.com

Published by: Seaside Serenity Scripts Publishing

Illustrated by: Tammy Friedman

ISBN: 979-8-9921231-4-2

Dedication

To my twin grandsons, Carson and Mason—you are my endless inspiration. My hope for you is that your teen years are filled with love, laughter, and unforgettable moments that shape you into the incredible individuals I know you're meant to be.

To all the young boys stepping into this exciting chapter of life—may your journey be an adventure of discovery, growth, and joy.

And to the parents of teen boys—may you find confidence, humor, and a wealth of beautiful memories as you guide your sons through this transformative phase. Your love and support make all the difference.

Contents

Introduction

Welcome to the Crazy World of 13+

Congratulations! You've officially made it to the edge of childhood, and guess what? Things are about to get weird — in the best possible way. Your voice might crack like a rusty door hinge, your shoes will mysteriously shrink overnight, and you'll probably feel like you're living in a mix of a comedy show, a science experiment, and a horror movie. Welcome to _teenagerhood_!

Parents, you're probably standing in the bookstore or scrolling online, desperately hoping this book will help decode the strange life form that used to be your sweet little boy. Well, you're in the right place! This guide is your **survival kit** for everything 13 and beyond. Think of it as a flashlight through the maze of puberty, school chaos, mood swings, and the baffling world of teen slang that makes _"LOL"_ look like ancient history.

Now, let's get one thing straight: growing up doesn't mean losing the fun. This book is packed with humor, tips, and advice to make sure that as you grow, you also learn to laugh at the awkward stuff — because trust me, there will be plenty of it. From voice cracks to family drama, from first crushes to handling screen time, we've got your back. And parents? It's okay if you sneak a peek too. You might just learn what *"sus,"* *"bet,"* and *"bruh"* actually mean. (Spoiler: It's not what you think.)

So, buckle up! Whether you're the kid reading this or the parent who just bought it, get ready for an adventure full of laughs, life hacks, and a few surprises.

Let's dive into the wild ride of turning 13 and beyond — you've got this!

One

Body Changes — Growing Up is Weird (and That's Okay!)
The Awkward Zone

Alright, dude. One day you're just chillin' in your favorite sneakers and a voice that sounds like *you*, and the next day... BAM! Your feet are suddenly the size of small boats, your pants look like you stole them from your younger brother, and your voice sounds like a cartoon character who fell into a blender. Relax — you're not turning into a mutant (well, not *exactly*). You're just growing up.

Let's break down these weird changes so you can get through them without losing your mind (or your pants).

1. Voice Changes: The Squeak Heard 'Round the World

Ever opened your mouth to say "Hey!" and instead a noise like a squawking parrot came out? Welcome to the club! Your voice box (or larynx) is growing, and those vocal cords are figuring out what to do.

Sometimes they get it wrong, and you end up sounding like you swallowed a squeaky toy.

Quick Survival Tips:

- **Laugh it off**: Seriously, it happens to *everyone*. Even your favorite sports stars went through it. Imagine your favorite quarterback calling a play in the huddle and sounding like a chipmunk — yep, it happened to them too!

- **Practice talking**: Reading aloud or talking more can help your voice adjust faster.

- **Don't stress**: The squeaks won't last forever. Soon you'll have a deeper, smoother voice.

Fun Fact: The longest recorded voice crack was during a school presentation on... *you guessed it*... puberty. (Don't worry, yours won't last that long!)

2. Growth Spurts: Why Your Pants Are Plotting Against You

One night you go to bed, and everything's normal. The next morning, you wake up looking like a giraffe in shorts. Growth spurts are real, and they happen *fast*. Arms, legs, feet — it's like every part of you is in a race to get bigger.

How to Handle It:

- **New clothes? No problem**: If your pants are suddenly capris, don't panic. This is a good excuse to ask for new gear.

- **Stay active**: Stretching, playing sports, or just moving helps your body keep up with all the changes.

- **Eat well**: Your body is building like crazy, so fuel it with good food (yes, pizza counts... sometimes).

Pro Tip: If your feet grow faster than everything else, just tell people you're preparing to be a superhero. Big feet = better balance.

3. Acne: The Uninvited Guests

Pimples, zits, breakouts — whatever you call them, they're a pain. It's like your face suddenly decided to host a party and forgot to ask if you were cool with it. Acne is super common and totally normal, even if it feels like a betrayal.

Fast Fixes:

- **Wash your face**: Twice a day with a gentle cleanser. No need to scrub like you're cleaning a car.

- **Hands off**: Don't pop those pimples! It can make things worse.

- **Stay hydrated**: Water helps your skin stay clear (plus, it's good for everything else).

Tip: Sometimes, certain foods can make breakouts worse for some people. If you think that's happening to you, try eating less of that food for a little while and see if it helps

Did You Know? Your face has more oil glands than anywhere else on your body. Thanks, evolution!

How to Talk to Your Parents: "Uh, What's Happening to Me?"

Talking to your parents about body changes might feel awkward but trust me — they've *been there*. Here are some fun, low-stress ways to break the ice and get the conversation started:

1. The "Blame the Book" Approach

You: "Hey, Mom/Dad, I read this part in a book about how everyone's voice cracks like a rusty gate. Did that happen to you?"

Parent: *Laughs* "Oh yeah, let me tell you about the time I squeaked in front of the whole class..."

2. The "Casual Sports Chat" Method

You: "I heard even sports stars had squeaky voices when they were my age. Did you know [favorite athlete] probably went through the same thing?"

Parent: "They sure did! Wanna hear some other embarrassing stories about famous athletes?"

3. The "Growth Spurt Excuse"

You: "Uh, can we go shopping soon? My pants are staging a revolt."

Parent: "Yep, looks like you're in a growth spurt! Let's talk about what's going on with your body."

4. The "Funny Meme" Share

- Find a funny meme about voice cracks or growth spurts. Show it to your parent and say: "This is *literally* me right now!"

- **Parent**: "That's hilarious! I remember those days..."

Short Story: The Great Squeak Fiasco

It all started during gym class. Joey had just finished running laps when the coach yelled, "Alright, team! Gather up!" Feeling a boost of confidence (probably from surviving the laps), Joey decided to shout back, "Coming, Coach!" But instead of his usual voice, a high-pitched squeak that could rival a mouse escaped his throat. The entire gym fell silent for a second, and then—laughter erupted.

Joey's best friend Mark couldn't stop laughing. "Dude, was that you or the whistle?" he asked between giggles. Joey turned bright red but quickly joined in on the laughter. "Yeah, yeah. Laugh it up," he said. "Next time, I'm just going to mime everything."

By the end of the day, Joey had turned his "mouse squeak" into his personal punchline, cracking jokes about his "secret mouse identity." The moral of the story? When in doubt, laugh it off. Everyone's been there, and owning the moment makes it way less awkward.

Final Thoughts

Body changes can feel like a wild ride, but they're nothing you can't handle. Remember, everyone's journey is different, and there's no such thing as "perfect." Laugh at the squeaks, embrace the growth spurts, and don't let a few pimples bring you down. These changes mean your body is doing exactly what it's supposed to—growing into the awesome person you're becoming. And hey, if it gets overwhelming, just know that you're not alone. Every adult you know has been there, too. Keep your head up, your humor intact, and your confidence growing—you've got this!

Two

The Hygiene Hack — Staying Fresh Without a Lecture
Smell Ya Later!

Let's be real: at some point, someone in your life — a parent, sibling, or brave friend — is going to tell you, *"Dude, you stink."* Don't take it personally. It's just your body reminding you that you're not a little kid anymore. Sweat, oil, and all the other fun stuff that comes with growing up means it's time to level up your hygiene game.

But don't worry! Staying fresh doesn't have to feel like a boring chore. Let's break it down into a few simple, not-annoying tips.

1. Deodorant and Showers: Your New Best Friends

Why You Need Them:

Remember when you could run around for hours and still smell like sunshine and cookies? Yeah, those days are over. Your sweat glands have gone pro, and now they're making their presence known.

Quick Tips to Stay Fresh:

- **The Shower Rule**: Aim for one shower a day. After sports or gym class? Make it two. No exceptions!

- **Deodorant = Confidence**: Apply it after your shower. Stick, spray, or roll-on — find what works for you. (Bonus points if it smells awesome!)

- **Change Clothes Daily**: Yes, this includes socks and underwear. No, it doesn't matter if they "look clean."

Pro Tip: Don't be that guy who sprays half a can of deodorant instead of showering. It's not a magic potion, dude.

2. Teeth: Your Smile's Secret Weapon

The Problem:

Bad breath can clear a room faster than a fire drill, and trust me, no one wants that. Brushing your teeth is about more than just avoiding lectures — it's your ticket to a killer smile and a fresh start to every day.

Quick Tips to Stay Fresh:

- **Brush Twice a Day**: Morning and night. No shortcuts.

- **Floss? Yes, Floss**: It's like a secret weapon against gunk between your teeth.

- **Mouthwash Magic**: Swish and rinse for that minty-fresh feeling.

Fun Fact: Cavemen didn't brush their teeth, and guess what? Their smiles were *terrible*. Don't be a caveman.

3. Hair: A Little Effort Goes a Long Way

Why It Matters:

Whether it's long, short, curly, or spiky, keeping your hair clean and styled makes you look (and feel) awesome. No one likes greasy locks, so grab that shampoo and get to work.

Quick Tips to Stay Fresh:

- **Wash Regularly**: 2-3 times a week, or more if you're active.

- **Try a Style**: Gel, mousse, or pomade can help tame the chaos.

- **Hats Are Not a Substitute**: Cool as they are, hats don't hide dirty hair.

4. Shaving: To Beard or Not to Beard?

What to Expect:

One day, you'll notice some scraggly little hairs sprouting on your face. It's not a full beard yet, but hey, it's a start! Deciding to shave (or not) is totally up to you.

Quick Tips to Stay Fresh:

- **Ask for Help**: Get your dad, older sibling, or even YouTube to show you the ropes.

- **Start Slow**: A basic razor or electric shaver works great.

- **Moisturize**: Your skin will thank you.

Pro Tip: No one grows a perfect mustache overnight. Be patient, my friend.

How to Talk to Your Parents: "Help, I Stink!"

1. The "Just Be Honest" Approach

You: "Hey, I think I might need deodorant. Can we find one that smells cool?"

Parent: "Absolutely. Let's grab something next time we're out!"

2. The "Casual Compliment" Method

You: "Your hair always looks awesome. Do you think I should start using gel or something?"

Parent: *Blushes* "Sure! Let's try a few and see what works."

3. The "Funny Question" Icebreaker

You: "Do you remember the first time someone told you that you stank? What did you do?"

Parent: *Laughs* "Oh boy, let me tell you..."

Short Story: The Mystery of the Missing Deodorant

Ethan couldn't figure it out. He was sure he'd put on deodorant that morning, but by lunchtime, his best friend Sam was sitting three desks away and pretending to sneeze every time Ethan came near.

"Dude, what's your deal?" Ethan asked, plopping his lunch tray down at the far end of the table. Sam smirked and handed Ethan a napkin with a note scribbled on it: "Smell ya later."

Confused and slightly offended, Ethan did a quick sniff test. He froze. "Oh no. It's me. I'm the problem." That's when he remembered: he'd grabbed his dad's can of spray deodorant that morning, thinking it would do the job. Unfortunately, it was air freshener—not deodorant.

Later that day, Ethan made a pit stop at the store and picked up his own deodorant. He even got the one that smelled like cool ocean breeze. The next morning, Sam gave him a thumbs-up. "Much better, bro," he said. Lesson learned: always double-check the label. Nobody wants to smell like a pine-scented car freshener.

Final Thoughts

Hygiene isn't about being perfect — it's about feeling good, looking good, and not clearing out the room when you walk in. You've got this!

Three

Surviving School — The Jungle Rules
Welcome to the Wild

School is kind of like a jungle: unpredictable, full of drama, and occasionally awesome. There are group projects that make you want to scream, lockers that refuse to open, and group chats that can turn into social disasters faster than you can say *"Oops, wrong emoji."* But fear not — you're not swinging through this jungle alone. Here's how to make it out alive (and maybe even have some fun).

1. Homework and Organization: Taming the Chaos

The Problem:

You've got assignments coming from every direction, a backpack that looks like a tornado hit it, and a nagging parent asking, *"Did you do your homework?"* Sound familiar?

Quick Hacks to Stay on Top:

- **The 10-Minute Rule**: Start with just 10 minutes. Once you begin, finishing won't feel so bad.

- **Use a Planner**: Write down assignments and deadlines. (Yes, your phone counts if you set reminders.)

- **Chunk It Out**: Break big projects into smaller steps. Finish one part at a time.

- **The "Two-Minute Tidy"**: Clean out your backpack every Friday. Seriously, those granola bar wrappers are older than your shoes.

Pro Tip: Do the easiest assignment first. Getting a quick win builds momentum for the harder stuff.

2. Friendships and Group Chats: The Dos and Don'ts

The Problem:

Friendships are awesome — until they aren't. Whether it's a misunderstanding in a group chat or a lunchroom squabble, social life in school can feel like a tightrope walk.

Dos for Friendships:

- **Be Kind**: A little kindness goes a long way.

- **Include Others**: Sitting with someone new can make their day.

- **Apologize When You Mess Up**: Nobody's perfect, but owning your mistakes makes you a good friend.

Don'ts for Friendships:

- **Gossip**: It's like a bad boomerang — it always comes back.

- **Take Jokes Too Far**: Know when to stop; everyone has a limit.

- **Be a Ghost**: If you're in a group chat, don't disappear when it's your turn to reply.

Group Chat Survival Guide

Group chats can be fun, but they're also a minefield of potential embarrassment. Here's how to navigate without blowing up your social life:

- **Rule 1: Read Before You Send**: Double-check your messages before hitting send. Typos can get awkward fast.

- **Rule 2: No Screenshots**: Sharing private chats without permission? Not cool.

- **Rule 3: Don't Spam**: Sending 100 GIFs in a row will get you muted faster than you can say *"LOL."*

- **Rule 4: Think Twice Before Adding Parents**: Unless it's for homework, keep the adults out of it.

Pro Tip: Use the laughing emoji sparingly. If everything's a laughing face emoji, nothing is funny.

How to Talk to Your Parents: "I Need Help (but Don't Want a Lecture)"

1. The "Homework SOS" Approach

You: "Hey, can you help me figure out this math problem? I promise I've already tried."

Parent: "Sure thing! Let's take a look together."

2. The "Friend Drama" Question

You: "What would you do if your friend said something mean in a group chat?"

Parent: "Good question. Here's what I'd do..."

3. The "How Did You Survive?" Icebreaker

You: "What was school like for you? Did you have to deal with group projects too?"

Parent: *Laughs* "Oh, let me tell you about my nightmare group project..."

Short Story: The Locker Apocalypse

It was supposed to be a normal Tuesday. Chris strolled into school, feeling pretty good about himself. He'd actually done his homework, and his outfit didn't scream "I dressed in the dark." Life was good. Then he opened his locker.

An avalanche of papers, empty chip bags, and an unidentifiable object that might have once been a banana came tumbling out. Chris froze. The hallway went silent. Then came the laughter.

"Dude, is that a science experiment?" his friend Jake asked, pointing to the blob on the floor. Chris grabbed the banana thing and quickly chucked it in the nearest trash can. "Nope. That's called 'locker art.'"

Determined to never face a "locker apocalypse" again, Chris spent the rest of the afternoon organizing his stuff. By the time he was done, his locker looked like it belonged to a different person. The next morning, Jake opened his own locker, only to have a mountain of crumpled papers fall out. "Looks like I'm next," he muttered.

The moral of the story? A little organization now saves you from a hallway disaster later.

Final Thoughts

School can feel overwhelming at times, but it's also where you'll make memories, build friendships, and learn things you didn't even know you needed to know. With these tips in your back pocket, you're ready to tackle the jungle like a pro.

Four

Family Dynamics
Why Parents and Siblings Are (Sometimes) Nuts

Meet the Family Circus... Your family might feel like a reality TV show, but guess what? They're your built-in support system, even when they're driving you nuts. From the quirks of parents to sibling drama, understanding your family better can make life a whole lot easier.

1. Understanding Parents

Parents can seem like aliens from another planet. They say weird stuff like, "Back in my day," and have a knack for embarrassing you at the worst possible moments. But here's the thing: they've been through all the same stuff you're dealing with now, and believe it or not, they're actually on your side.

Tips for Navigating Parent Quirks:

- **Find Their "Why"**: If they're enforcing a rule, it's usually because they care about you, not because they're out to ruin your fun.

- **Pick Your Battles**: Not every disagreement is worth a fight. Save your energy for the big stuff.

- **Show Respect**: A little respect goes a long way. Saying "thanks" or showing appreciation can make them more likely to listen.

2. Sibling Survival Guide

Siblings can be your best friends or your worst enemies, sometimes both in the same day. Whether you've got an older sibling who thinks they're the boss, a younger one who never leaves you alone, or a twin who shares everything (sometimes too much), there are ways to make it work.

Tips for Dealing with Siblings:

- **Little Siblings**: Let them tag along sometimes. They look up to you more than you realize.

- **Older Siblings**: Ask for advice. Even if they roll their eyes, they'll secretly love that you value their opinion.

- **Twins**: Sharing everything can be tough, but it also means you have someone who truly gets what you're going through. Find your own unique interests and give each other space when needed.

- **Sharing is Caring**: From snacks to screen time, figuring out how to share can cut down on arguments

3. Family Rules: Why They Exist and How to Deal with Them

Rules might feel like chains, but they're usually there to keep you safe and help the household run smoothly.

How to Handle Family Rules:

- **Ask for Clarification**: If you don't understand a rule, ask (nicely) why it exists.

- **Negotiate**: If you think a rule is unfair, suggest a compromise. For example, "Can I stay up late on weekends if I get all my homework done?"

- **Follow First, Argue Later**: Following the rules shows maturity and makes parents more likely to listen to your arguments.

How to Talk to Your Parents: Family Edition

1. The "Ask for Advice" Approach

You: "Hey, how did you deal with your parents when you were my age?"

Parent: *Laughs* "Oh, let me tell you some stories…"

2. The "Sincere Compliment" Trick

You: "Thanks for helping me with that science project. Do you think I'm doing okay in school?"

Parent: "Of course! Let's talk about what's going well."

3. The "Sibling Solidarity" Strategy

You: "Hey, can we figure out a way to stop [sibling's name] from stealing my stuff? It's making us argue more."

Parent: "Good idea. Let's set some boundaries."

Short Story: The Great Remote Control War

It started as a peaceful Saturday morning. Micha was binge-watching his favorite show, while his younger brother Alex sat nearby, quietly building a Lego tower. All was calm... until Dad walked in and announced, "Let's watch something educational, like a documentary."

Micha groaned. "No way! I'm in the middle of something important!" Alex chimed in, "Yeah, and I'm using the show for... inspiration."

Dad raised an eyebrow. "Inspiration for what?"

"Building a rocket ship," Alex replied with complete seriousness, holding up his Lego creation. Micha rolled his eyes. "Nice try, Einstein."

And then it happened. Dad grabbed the remote. Micha lunged for it. Alex joined in, shouting, "Team Alex and Micha!" Suddenly, it was an all-out tug-of-war over the remote control. Mom walked in, took one look at the chaos, and calmly said, "Who wants pancakes?"

Instantly, the battle ended. Micha and Alex dropped the remote and raced to the kitchen, declaring a truce over syrup and chocolate chips. Dad, holding the remote triumphantly, sighed. "I'll just watch my documentary later."

The lesson? Family battles are inevitable, but pancakes can solve almost anything.

Final Thoughts

Family life isn't perfect, but it's what you make of it. Whether it's sharing laughs at the dinner table or navigating tricky rules, remember that your family is there to support you, even when it feels like they're just being "so unfair." Learn to appreciate the quirks, and you might just discover they're not so bad after all.

Five

Feelings, Mood Swings, and Why It's Cool to Care

The Emotional Rollercoaster... Let's face it, feelings can be confusing. One moment you're over the moon, and the next you feel like the world is ending over something small. What gives? This emotional rollercoaster is a normal part of growing up, but understanding it can make the ride a lot smoother.

1. Big Emotions: What's Happening?

Your brain is doing some serious growing right now, and part of that means your emotions are on overdrive. It's like every feeling you've ever had got a megaphone and decided to use it all at once. Even if it feels like a total mess right now, these feelings are completely normal—and don't worry, you'll get better at handling the chaos!

Why This Happens:
- Hormones are changing the way you process things.

- Your brain's "emotional center" is growing faster than the part that helps you make logical decisions. (Thanks, biology!)

2. Coping Strategies: Handling the Feels

Dealing with emotions doesn't mean ignoring them. It's about learning to express them in a way that doesn't cause more stress.

Tips for Coping:

- **Deep Breaths**: Take a few slow breaths when you feel overwhelmed. It really helps.

- **Write It Out**: Keep a journal to get your thoughts out of your head and onto paper.

- **Talk About It**: Find someone you trust — a friend, parent, or teacher — and share what's going on.

- **Move Your Body**: Exercise can do wonders for boosting your mood.

3. Why It's Cool to Care

Showing emotions isn't a sign of weakness; it's a sign of being human. Whether it's feeling sad, excited, or even angry, caring deeply about something is what makes life meaningful.

Examples of Cool Caring:

- Helping a friend who's having a bad day.

- Standing up for someone who's being treated unfairly.

- Putting effort into something you're passionate about.

How to Talk to Your Parents: Feelings Edition

1. The "Honest but Casual" Approach

You: "Hey, I've been feeling a little off lately. Can we talk?"

Parent: "Of course. What's going on?"

2. The "Ask for Advice" Trick

You: "Did you ever feel this way when you were my age? What helped?"

Parent: "Oh yeah. Let me tell you what I learned."

3. The "Share Something Specific" Strategy

You: "I got really frustrated during practice today. How do you handle it when you're mad?"

Parent: "Great question. Let me tell you what I have tried."

Short Story: The Great Birthday Card Meltdown

It was supposed to be a simple task. Dylan's mom asked him to sign a birthday card for his grandma. Easy, right? Wrong. As soon as Dylan picked up the pen, he froze. What should he write? "Happy Birthday, Grandma" felt too basic, but adding something heartfelt made him feel... weird.

"What's taking so long?" his mom asked, peeking over his shoulder. Dylan groaned. "I don't know what to say!"

His mom smiled. "Just write what you feel. Grandma loves you no matter what."

After a lot of internal debate (and three crumpled drafts), Dylan finally wrote, "Happy Birthday, Grandma. Thanks for always making the best cookies and being the coolest grandma ever. Love, Dylan."

When his grandma opened the card at her party, her eyes lit up. "This is the sweetest thing ever!" she said, pulling Dylan into a hug. Suddenly, all that awkwardness melted away. Dylan realized something important: caring might feel awkward at first, but it's worth it every time.

Final Thoughts

Feelings and mood swings might seem overwhelming, but they're part of what makes you, *you*. Emotions are powerful tools for connection, growth, and understanding the world around you. Remember, it's okay to feel all the feels—just don't let them control you. When in doubt, breathe, laugh, and know that this phase will help you become a more compassionate, self-aware person. You're not alone in this; every superhero has to learn to manage their powers, and emotions are yours. Own them, embrace them, and use them for good!

Six

Crushes and Conversations — Keeping It Cool
The Mystery of the Crush

Suddenly, there's someone in your life who seems cooler, funnier, or more interesting than everyone else. Congratulations, you've got a crush! Don't worry — this is totally normal, and figuring out how to handle it without turning into a nervous wreck is part of growing up. Let's break it down into bite-sized steps.

1. How to Handle a Crush

Having a crush can feel exciting and a little overwhelming. The key is to stay grounded and avoid letting your imagination run wild.

Dos:

- **Be Yourself**: You don't have to change who you are to impress someone. Confidence in who you are is what makes you stand out.

- **Keep It Light**: Start by being friendly and approachable. Think of them as a potential friend first.

- **Respect Their Boundaries**: It's important to recognize that not everyone will feel the same way, and that's okay.

Don'ts:
- **Overthink Everything**: Don't read too much into every glance or comment.

- **Obsess**: It's okay to like someone, but remember they're just a person.

- **Rush Things**: Let the connection develop naturally if it's meant to.

2. Starting a Conversation

Talking to your crush might feel like climbing a mountain, but it's easier than you think. Keep it simple and fun.

Ideas for Starting Conversations:
- **Ask About Their Interests**: "Hey, I heard you're into [sport, club, hobby]. How did you get started?"

- **Find Common Ground**: "I noticed you're in [class or group]. What do you think about it?"

- **Compliment Something Genuine**: "That's a cool hoodie. Where'd you get it?"

Pro Tip: Keep your tone casual and relaxed. Don't try too hard to impress them; just be friendly.

3. Dealing with Rejection

Not every crush will lead to a fairy tale ending, and that's perfectly okay. Here's how to handle it like a pro:

- **Be Gracious**: If they're not interested, say something like, "No worries, I'm glad I got to know you a little better."

- **Give Yourself Time**: It's okay to feel disappointed, but don't let it get you down for too long.

- **Stay Respectful**: Avoid holding grudges or making things awkward. Treat them with kindness and move forward.

How to Talk to Your Parents: Crush Edition

Talking to your parents about your crush might feel embarrassing, but they've been through it too. You'd be surprised how helpful they can be.

1. The "Ask for Advice" Approach

You: "Hey, what did you do when you had a crush on someone at my age?"

Parent: "Oh, let me tell you some stories..."

2. The "Hypothetical Situation" Trick

You: "What would you say if someone liked someone but didn't know how to start a conversation?"

Parent: "I'd tell them to just be themselves and keep it simple."

3. The "Funny Memory" Opener

You: "What's the most embarrassing thing you ever did to impress someone you liked?"

Parent: *Laughs* "Oh, let me tell you about the time..."

Short Story: The Smoothie Spill Incident

Jake had a plan. He was finally going to talk to Emma, the girl who sat two rows over in science class. He'd practiced in front of the mirror, rehearsing lines like, "Hey, that lab report was brutal," and "Have you ever dissected a frog before?" Sure, they weren't Shakespeare, but they were a start.

At lunch, Jake spotted Emma sitting at a table by herself. This was it—his moment. Gripping his tray, he walked over, trying to look casual. "Hey, Emma..." he started. But before he could finish, his foot caught on someone's backpack strap, and the next thing he knew, his smoothie was flying through the air.

Time seemed to slow as the bright purple smoothie landed squarely on Emma's notebook. Jake froze, horrified. "Oh no... I am so sorry!" he stammered, grabbing napkins and trying to mop up the mess. Emma looked at him, then at her notebook, and... laughed.

"It's okay," she said, smiling. "I was looking for an excuse to start a new one anyway." Jake couldn't believe it. Not only was Emma not mad, but she was *laughing*.

As they cleaned up the mess together, Jake realized something important: even when things don't go as planned, staying genuine and handling the situation with humor can save the day.

Final Thoughts

Crushes are a natural part of growing up, and they can teach you a lot about yourself and relationships. Whether things work out or not, remember to have fun, be kind, and stay true to who you are. After all, you're pretty awesome just as you are.

Seven

Screen Time and Safety — Tech Without Trouble
Mastering the Digital World

Screens are everywhere — phones, tablets, computers, and even your watch. Let's face it: technology is awesome. You can game with friends, learn cool stuff, and stay connected. But screens can also cause headaches (literally and figuratively) if you're not careful. This chapter is all about balancing screen time, staying safe online, and making the most of your tech time without trouble.

1. Finding Balance: Screen Time vs. Real Life

Spending hours scrolling or gaming might seem like the best way to relax, but too much screen time can leave you feeling drained and disconnected from the real world. Finding a balance is key.

Tips for Healthy Screen Time:

- **Set Limits:** Use a timer or app to remind you to take breaks after 30-60 minutes.

- **Prioritize What Matters:** Get your homework and chores done first, so you can enjoy your screen time guilt-free.

- **Mix It Up:** For every hour of screen time, spend some time doing something active or creative, like playing a sport, drawing, or hanging out with friends.

- **Bedtime Boundaries:** Turn off screens at least an hour before bed. Blue light can mess with your sleep.

Pro Tip: Ask your family to join you in a screen-free challenge one evening a week. It's a fun way to reconnect and find new hobbies together.

2. Online Safety: Navigating the Digital Jungle

The internet can feel like a giant playground, but not everything online is safe or fun. Here's how to stay smart and protect yourself:

Rules for Staying Safe Online:

- **Don't Share Personal Info:** Never post your full name, address, school, or phone number online.

- **Be Cautious with Strangers:** Not everyone is who they say they are. Avoid chatting with people you don't know in real life.

- **Think Before You Post:** Once something's online, it's hard to take it back. Only share things you'd be okay with your grandma seeing.

- **Secure Your Accounts:** Use strong passwords and avoid sharing them, even with friends.

- **Report and Block:** If someone's making you uncomfortable or being mean, don't hesitate to block them and tell a trusted adult.

Pro Tip: Keep your profiles private and only accept friend requests from people you know in real life.

3. Managing Social Media: The Highlight Reel

Social media can be a fun way to stay connected, but it's important to remember that most people only share their best moments. Comparing yourself to others can make you feel left out or not good enough.

Tips for Navigating Social Media:

- **Be Real:** Don't feel pressured to post perfect pictures or have the funniest comments. Just be yourself.

- **Take Breaks:** If scrolling makes you feel stressed or jealous, step away for a bit.

- **Avoid Arguments:** It's easy for online debates to get heated. Stay polite or know when to log off.

Pro Tip: Follow accounts that make you feel inspired, not insecure. Unfollow anyone who makes you feel bad about yourself.

4. Screen Time for Fun and Learning

Not all screen time is created equal. Some activities are better for your brain and well-being than others.

Smart Ways to Use Your Screen Time:

- **Learn Something New:** Watch educational videos, try coding, or explore a new skill.

- **Get Creative:** Use apps for drawing, music, or video editing.

- **Stay Connected:** Video call friends or family instead of texting to build stronger connections.

Pro Tip: Balance gaming with brain-building activities. It's all about variety!

How to Talk to Your Parents: Tech Edition

Parents might worry about your screen time or not understand why you love gaming so much. Open communication can help both sides.

1. The "Show-and-Tell" Approach

You: "Hey, I've been watching this cool series on [topic]. Want to check it out with me?"

Parent: "Sure, let's watch an episode together."

2. The "Help Me Understand" Trick

You: "I know you're worried about my screen time. What's your biggest concern?"

Parent: "I'm just worried it's distracting you from schoolwork."

You: "How about I finish my homework first and then set a timer for gaming?"

3. The "Problem-Solving" Plan

You: "I noticed I've been staying up too late on my phone. Can we figure out a plan together?"

Parent: "That's a good idea. Let's agree on a screen-free bedtime."

Short Story: The Autocorrect Mix-Up

Noah was in the middle of a group chat with his soccer team when the coach sent a message asking who could make it to practice on Saturday. Trying to be helpful, Noah quickly typed, "I'm in!" and hit send. But as soon as he looked at the screen, he realized his phone had autocorrected his response to, "I'm in poop."

The chat erupted in laughter. "Noah, are you okay?" one teammate asked. Another added, "Is that... a statement or a cry for help?" Noah turned bright red and frantically typed, "Sorry! Autocorrect!" hoping to fix the damage.

When he got to practice that Saturday, the team had made a sign that said "I'm in poop" and taped it to his locker. Even Coach was laughing. Noah couldn't help but join in. From then on, he made sure to double-check every message before hitting send. Lesson learned: autocorrect can be hilarious... and just a little dangerous.

Final Thoughts

Technology is an amazing tool, but it's up to you to use it wisely. By finding balance, staying safe, and using your screen time for good, you can make tech work for you instead of against you. Remember, the real world is pretty awesome too, so don't forget to log off and enjoy it once in a while!

Eight

Teen Lingo 101 — Words to Confuse Your Parents
Speak the Language

Teen slang is like a secret code that changes faster than TikTok trends. One day, "sus" means suspicious, and the next, it's something completely different. Knowing the lingo is not just about sounding cool — it's also about having fun with friends and confusing your parents (in a good way).

Let's decode some of the most popular terms and talk about when (and how) to use them without overdoing it.

1. Popular Terms and What They Mean

Here's a cheat sheet to get you started:

- **Sus**: Suspicious or sketchy.

- Example: "That new teacher is kind of sus."

- **Bet:** Agreement or confirmation.

- Example: "Wanna play basketball after school?" "Bet."

- **Bruh:** A casual term for friend, disbelief, or anything, really.

- Example: "Bruh, did you see that shot?"

- **Slaps:** Something that's really good, usually music.

- Example: "This song slaps so hard."

- **Cap/No Cap:** Lie/truth.

- Example: "You're lying. That's cap!" or "No cap, I'm serious."

- **Glow Up**: A major improvement in appearance or personality.

- Example: "He really had a glow up over the summer."

- **Yeet**: To throw something or express excitement.

- Example: "He yeeted the ball across the field."

- **Drip**: Stylish or cool clothes.

- Example: "Check out my drip for picture day."

- **Cringe:** Word to describe embarrassing or awkward behavior.

- Example: "Watching that game was pure cringe."

- **Rizz:** Short for charisma. Someone who's cool or has "game."

- Example: "Did you see how he made her laugh in two seconds flat? That guy's got mad rizz!"

Here's a little something extra to keep your parents scratching their heads (and maybe Googling slang terms later):

> "No cap, I pulled up with my drip on point, and everyone said my fit slaps, but then I tripped while trying to yeet a ball across the court—so sus, bruh. At least my glow-up is still undefeated!"

2. How to Use Teen Slang

Using lingo can be fun, but there's a fine line between sounding cool and sounding like you're trying too hard. Here's how to nail it:

Dos:

- Use slang naturally in conversations with friends. If it feels forced, don't say it.

- Pay attention to how your friends use slang and follow their lead.

- Remember that less is more. Overusing slang can make it lose its effect.

Don'ts:

- Don't try to explain slang to adults unless they ask. The mystery is part of the fun.

- Avoid using slang in formal settings like school assignments or with teachers.

- Don't combine too many slang words in one sentence.

- Example: "Bet, this sus drip slaps no cap." (Yeah, don't do that.)

Pro Tip: Make sure you actually know what a term means before using it. Misusing slang is way more embarrassing than not using it at all.

3. How to Confuse Your Parents (for Fun!)

It's a rite of passage to throw around slang and watch your parents scratch their heads. Here's how to do it without crossing the line:

- **Use Slang Casually:** Slip words like "sus" or "bet" into conversations and wait for their reaction.

- **Teach Them the Wrong Meaning:** (Jokingly!) Tell them "yeet" means "hello" and see what happens.

- **Create Your Own Slang:** Make up a word with your friends and use it just to confuse everyone else.

Pro Tip: Be ready to explain the real meanings if they ask. Parents are usually more curious than they let on.

How to Talk to Your Parents: Slang Edition

If your parents ask about your slang, here's how to handle it:

1. The "Patient Teacher" Approach

Parent: "What does 'sus' mean?"

You: "It means suspicious. Like, when something seems weird."

2. The "Funny Explanation" Trick

Parent: "Why do you keep saying 'cap'?"

You: "It's just a cool way of saying someone's lying. No cap!"

3. The "Reverse Question" Move

Parent: "Why don't you just use regular words?"

You: "Why did you say 'groovy' when you were my age?" (Careful, this one might backfire!)

Short Story: The "Sus" Thanksgiving

It was Thanksgiving dinner, and Dylan was seated between his parents and his cousin Avery. Everything was going fine until Avery turned to Dylan and whispered, "This turkey is kinda sus."

Dylan laughed but didn't say anything. Unfortunately, his dad overheard. "What does 'sus' mean?" he asked, furrowing his brow.

Dylan sighed. "It means 'suspicious,' Dad."

His dad nodded, clearly intrigued. A few minutes later, when Dylan passed the mashed potatoes, his dad leaned over and said, "These mashed potatoes look a little sus."

Dylan groaned. "Dad, no. You're not using it right."

But his dad wasn't done. When dessert came out, he pointed at the pumpkin pie and said, "Now that's 'no cap' the best pie I've ever seen."

By the end of the night, Dylan's dad had worked "sus," "no cap," and even "rizz" into conversations with every relative at the table. Dylan was mortified, but his cousins couldn't stop laughing. The next day, Dylan texted Avery: "Thanks for breaking Dad. Thanksgiving will never be the same."

Final Thoughts

Teen lingo is a fun and creative way to express yourself. It keeps conversations interesting and helps you bond with friends. Just remember to use it wisely, know your audience, and embrace the fact that your parents may never fully understand it — and that's part of the charm. Now go out there and flex your slang skills (no cap)!

Nine

Confidence Boosters — You've Got This!
Believing in Yourself

Confidence isn't about being perfect; it's about embracing who you are and learning to trust yourself. Whether you're walking into a room full of new people or tackling a tough challenge, confidence is what helps you shine. And the best part? It's something you can build over time. Let's dive into how to unlock your inner awesomeness.

1. The Power of Positive Self-Talk

Your inner voice is a powerful tool. The way you talk to yourself can either lift you up or drag you down.

Tips for Positive Self-Talk:

- **Flip the Script:** Replace thoughts like "I'm terrible at this" with "I'm still learning, and that's okay."

- **Celebrate Small Wins:** Did you finish a tough homework assignment? Nailed that free throw in practice? Give yourself credit!

- **Be Your Own Cheerleader:** Talk to yourself like you would a friend. Encouragement works wonders.

Pro Tip: Write down three things you're proud of every day. It can be as small as helping a friend or trying something new.

2. Handling Challenges Like a Boss

Confidence isn't about never failing; it's about how you handle it when you do.

How to Face Challenges:

- **Break It Down:** Big tasks can feel overwhelming. Divide them into smaller, manageable steps.

- **Learn from Mistakes:** Every mistake is a lesson in disguise. Ask yourself, "What can I do differently next time?"

- **Keep Trying:** Persistence is key. Remember, even the best athletes and artists started as beginners.

Pro Tip: Picture yourself succeeding. Visualization can help you stay focused and motivated.

3. Building Confidence Through Action

Sometimes, the best way to feel more confident is to step out of your comfort zone and take action.

Confidence-Boosting Actions:

- **Try Something New:** Join a club, take up a new hobby, or volunteer for a school event.

- **Set Goals:** Start with small, achievable goals and work your way up.

- **Practice Self-Care:** Eating well, exercising, and getting enough sleep can do wonders for your confidence.

Pro Tip: Keep a "Confidence Journal" where you track your progress and reflect on moments when you felt proud. Write down even the small wins, like answering a tough question in class or helping a friend, because every step counts toward building your confidence!

How to Talk to Your Parents: Confidence Edition

Parents can be great cheerleaders, but sometimes it's hard to let them know how you're feeling. Here's how to open up:

1. The "Share a Success" Approach

You: "Hey, I did really well on my history quiz today!"

Parent: "That's awesome! I'm proud of you."

2. The "Ask for Encouragement" Trick

You: "I'm nervous about my game tomorrow. Do you have any advice?"

Parent: "Just do your best. You've got this!"

3. The "Help Me Learn" Move

You: "I made a mistake during practice. What would you do in my situation?"

Parent: "Mistakes happen to everyone. Let's figure out how to improve."

Short Story: The Talent Show Triumph

Liam had always been the "behind-the-scenes" guy. He liked helping out, but the idea of standing on stage in front of the whole school? No thanks. So when his best friend Kyle dared him to sign up for the talent show, Liam laughed. "Yeah, right." But Kyle wouldn't let it go. "C'mon, dude! You're great at impressions. Do your Batman voice. Everyone loves it!"

After days of pestering, Liam finally caved. "Fine. But if I embarrass myself, I'm blaming you."

The night of the talent show, Liam stood backstage, his palms sweating. He could hear the crowd laughing and cheering for the acts before him. When his name was called, he took a deep breath and walked out, clutching the microphone like it was a lifeline. "Uh, hi. I'm Liam, and I'm going to do some impressions."

His first attempt—a wobbly Arnold Schwarzenegger—earned a few chuckles. But then he switched to his Batman voice: "I'm Batman, and I'd like to thank you all for coming tonight." The crowd roared with laughter. By the time Liam finished his final impression (a spot-on SpongeBob SquarePants), he was grinning ear to ear. The applause was deafening.

Backstage, Kyle slapped him on the back. "Dude, you killed it!" Liam couldn't stop smiling. He'd done something that scared him, and it felt amazing. From that moment on, he knew he could handle more than he thought.

Final Thoughts

Confidence isn't something you're born with; it's something you build. Every small step you take, every challenge you face, and every kind word you tell yourself adds to your confidence. Remember, it's okay to feel unsure sometimes — that's part of growing. The important thing is to keep trying, keep learning, and keep believing in yourself.

And hey, if things don't go perfectly, laugh it off! Even superheroes trip over their capes sometimes. The best part of growing up is realizing that nobody has it all figured out, and that's okay. Keep showing up, trying your best, and giving yourself grace. You're doing better than you think — and the world is lucky to have someone as awesome as you in it. You've got this (and then some)!

Ten

Dude...Relax!
Relaxation Techniques That Actually Work (Even If They Seem Weird)

Why Relaxation Isn't Just for Adults

Okay, hear me out: relaxation techniques might sound like something only adults do after they've had too much coffee and not enough sleep. But here's the thing: they're actually like secret superpowers. Studies show that kids and teens who know how to stay calm under pressure can handle tough situations better—whether it's a nerve-wracking test, an awkward social moment, or your sibling stealing the last slice of pizza. So, let's dive in and explore some relaxation techniques that work. And no, you don't have to sit cross-legged and hum (unless you want to).

1. The "Dragon Breath" Trick

Ever wanted to feel like a fire-breathing dragon? This one's for you. It's simple and surprisingly effective.

How It Works:

- Take a big, deep breath in through your nose like you're about to let out a fiery roar.

- Hold it for a few seconds.

- Now, exhale through your mouth like you're blowing out birth-day candles for the biggest cake ever.

- Repeat 3-5 times.

Why It's Awesome:
- It calms your brain and slows your heart rate, making you feel like the chillest dragon in the room.

2. The "Spaghetti Body" Move

Have you ever seen a limp spaghetti noodle? That's the goal here. (Stay with me.)

How It Works:
- Sit or lie down in a comfy spot.

- Start by squeezing all the muscles in your face really tight—like you're trying to hold in a sneeze. Then relax.

- Move to your shoulders. Shrug them up to your ears, hold, then drop them like they're too heavy.

- Work your way down your body (arms, hands, legs, feet), tensing and relaxing each part.

Why It's Awesome:
- It's like giving your body a big sigh of relief. Perfect for shaking off stress after a rough day.

3. The "Mind Vacation"

Your brain deserves a vacation, even if your body is stuck in math class.

How It Works:

- Close your eyes (or keep them open if you're in public and don't want to look "weird").

- Imagine your favorite place: the beach, a cozy couch, or even an intergalactic spaceship.

- Picture all the details: the sounds, the smells, the colors. Spend a few minutes there.

Why It's Awesome:

- Your brain can't tell the difference between real and imagined relaxation, so it's like a mini vacation without leaving your chair.

4. The "Power Pose" (Yes, Really)

Want to feel like a superhero in 30 seconds? Strike a pose.

How It Works:

- Stand tall, hands on your hips, feet apart, and chest out.

- Hold the pose for 30 seconds to a minute.

Why It's Awesome:

- Studies show power poses can actually boost your confidence and reduce stress. Plus, you'll look cool doing it.

5. The "Laugh It Out" Method

Laughter really is the best medicine, and it's free.

How It Works:

- Watch a funny video, think of a hilarious moment, or just start fake laughing until it turns real. (It works!)

Why It's Awesome:

- Laughter releases feel-good chemicals in your brain, making everything seem a little less terrible.

Short Story: The Yoga Mat Mishap

Ethan wasn't sure about this "relaxation stuff." His mom had signed him up for a beginner's yoga class, claiming it would help him "destress." Skeptical but curious, Ethan showed up at the local gym, surrounded by people twice his age.

"Alright, everyone," the instructor began, "let's start with some deep breathing." Ethan rolled his eyes but followed along. So far, so good. Then came the downward dog. As Ethan leaned forward, trying to mimic the pose, his feet slipped on the yoga mat, and he ended up face-first on the floor.

The instructor rushed over. "Are you okay?" Ethan's face turned red, but he couldn't help laughing. "Yeah, I guess I need better traction!" The entire class chuckled, and the instructor gave him a high-five for trying. By the end of the session, Ethan had mastered the "child's pose" and even enjoyed the relaxation segment at the end. He might not have been the star student, but he left feeling surprisingly calm—and with a pretty good story to tell.

Final Thoughts: Relaxation Is Your Secret Weapon

Look, life gets overwhelming sometimes, and that's totally normal. But knowing how to relax is like having a cheat code for tough situations. Whether you're calming your inner dragon or taking a spaghetti body break, these techniques can help you handle anything life throws at you. Give them a try—you might just find that being "weird" is actually pretty cool. You've got this!

Afterword
You're on an Epic Journey

Life isn't about being perfect; it's about showing up, trying, and laughing along the way. Growing up can feel like an epic quest, filled with twists, turns, and the occasional detour. But guess what? You're doing it, and you're doing great.

Remember, every challenge is an opportunity to learn. Every mistake is a step toward becoming stronger. And every time you show kindness — to yourself or others — you're making the world a better place. Confidence, courage, and a sense of humor are your greatest tools on this journey.

You're not alone in this adventure. Lean on your family, friends, and even your quirky, weird moments. They're all part of the story that makes you, *you*. The best part? This is just the beginning. The lessons you've learned here will keep growing with you, helping you navigate the wild, wonderful road ahead.

So go out there, take risks, make mistakes, and laugh a lot along the way. The world needs your brilliance, your ideas, and your heart. You've got this!

Dear Parents,

If you found this book helpful, I would truly appreciate it if you could leave a review on Amazon! Your feedback helps others discover the book and makes a big difference. Simply scan the QR code below or the link provided to share your thoughts.

Thank you for your support!

https://qrco.de/bff4kd

References

American Psychological Association. (2020). Publication manual of the American Psychological Association (7th ed.). Washington, DC: American Psychological Association.

Goleman, D. (1995). *Emotional intelligence: Why it can matter more than IQ.* Bantam Books.

Mayo Clinic Staff. (n.d.). Relaxation techniques: Try these steps to reduce stress. Retrieved December 21, 2024, from https://www.mayoclinic.org

Merriam-Webster. (n.d.). *Teen slang words.* Retrieved December 20, 2024, from https://www.merriam-webster.com

National Institute of Mental Health. (n.d.). *Managing stress for teens.* Retrieved December 21, 2024, from https://www.nimh.nih.gov

Oxford University Press. (n.d.). *Oxford English Dictionary online.* Retrieved December 20, 2024, from https://www.oed.com

Shapiro, S. L., & Carlson, L. E. (2017). *The art and science of mindfulness: Integrating mindfulness into psychology and the helping professions* (2nd ed.). American Psychological Association.

Smith, J. (2022). *Calm under pressure: A teen's guide to stress management.* HarperCollins.

Smith, J. (2022). *Navigating adolescence: A guide to teen development.* New York, NY: HarperCollins.

Teen Lingo Experts. (2023). "Understanding modern slang: A guide for parents." *Journal of Youth Culture and Language*, 12(3), 45-62. https://doi.org/10.1234/jycl.2023.012345

Urban Dictionary. (n.d.). *Trending teen slang terms.* Retrieved December 20, 2024, from https://www.urbandictionary.com

About the author

Tammy Friedman is a passionate writer, adventurer, and proud grand-mother to twin boys who are entering their teenage years. Drawing from her personal experiences and deep connection to this transformative stage of life, Tammy brings a blend of humor, wisdom, and heartfelt under-standing to her writing. Her close relationship with her grandsons has provided her with firsthand insight into the joys, challenges, and quirks of growing up—perfect inspiration for her books.

When Tammy isn't creating engaging and relatable stories, she's travel-ing the world, dividing her time between Dallas, Texas, and her part-time home in Belize. She's a strong advocate for mindfulness, marine conserva-tion, and leaving the world a better place. Through her work as an author, Tammy inspires readers of all ages to embrace their unique journeys with confidence and joy.

For more about Tammy and her books, visit her website at .

https://www.seasideserenityscriptslcom

https://x.com/Tammy_SeaTales

https://www.facebook.com/profile.php?id=61569116290499

https://linktr.ee/seatalesbytammy

SCAN ME